Route and Branch in Sussex

Sussex branch lines in the 1950s

Anthony Burges

Colourpoint Books

Route and Branch in Sussex

Dedicated to Jim Aston and Peter Baughan; old friends and Sussex residents, who continue in their different ways to enrich the study of railway history in Britain.

First Edition
First Impression

© Anthony Burges and Colourpoint Books 2008

Designed by Colourpoint Books
Printed by GPS Colour Graphics Ltd

ISBN 978 1 906578 14 5

Colourpoint Books
Colourpoint House
Jubilee Business Park
21 Jubilee Road
Newtownards
County Down
Northern Ireland
BT23 4YH
Tel: 028 9182 0505
Fax: 028 9182 1900
E-mail: info@colourpoint.co.uk
Web-site: www.colourpoint.co.uk

After an initial period as a 'mourner' in the fifties at branch line funerals in the UK and Ireland, Tony pursued studies at Southampton University followed by graduate school at Northwestern University, Chicago. His subsequent career in the Canadian government as Transport Policy Advisor in the Department of Finance, Director General, Grain Transportation & Handling, and subsequently Deputy Executive Director, Australian Railway Research & Development Organization earned him the sobriquet of 'Mr Branchline' among his colleagues. Retiring recently from a Washington DC based firm of transportation consultants he is now devoting his time to writing railway books in Ottawa. He is also the author of *Offshore on the Southern - The Isle of Wight railways in the 1950s and 1960s* published by Colourpoint Books.

Unless otherwise credited all photographs are by the author.

Front cover: Robertsbridge, associated by devotees with the manufacture of cricket bats, was revered by railway enthusiasts as a junction with the legendary Kent & East Sussex Light Railway. As Schools No 30925 *Cheltenham* approaches with a lengthy Charing Cross–Hastings train, one of Stroudley's renowned Terriers, No 32636, is shunting the solitary coach it has brought in from Tenterden Town. After some faltering starts the final chapter may not yet have been written on the saga of the Colonel Stephens heritage at Robertsbridge.

GR Siviour

Rear cover: An advantage of a 'private' train was that the friendly crew made photo stops as required. Such was this scene near Raughmere Farm on 27 May 1959, in which 32509 poses for posterity on the 'light weight' Lavant goods (full story, page 7).

Introduction

In the early fifties, the county of Sussex presented a railway scene vastly different from that of today. Its rail network was a mix of electrified main lines connecting coastal resorts to London, which were the domain of first generation Southern electric multiple units dating from the pre-World War II period, steam worked connecting routes that followed meandering paths across the difficult terrain of the Weald, plus several more traditional branch lines which were suffering a steady decline in passenger traffic as bus services and the private car provided increasingly attractive alternatives in terms of travel time and convenience. Steam locomotives of the pre grouping predecessors of the Southern Railway (the SE&CR, LB&SCR and the LSWR) and much of the passenger rolling stock, with a similar ancestry, were still in evidence. It was such a combination that conferred so much charm to the non-electrified lines that threaded an area of great natural beauty. Time seemed to have stood still in many of these railway backwaters.

This book does not purport to offer either a comprehensive or detailed history of the Sussex railways. Rather, it seeks to convey through photographs something of the flavour of a time fifty years past, by focusing on four categories of line. Firstly, a steam main line route, and more specifically, the section that extended south from Tunbridge Wells to the coastal resorts of St Leonards and Hastings. Secondly, my camera recorded the somewhat urbanized branch line that linked the Hastings main line at Crowhurst to Bexhill West. Branch lines in Sussex were characterized by a number of trans-Wealden secondary routes which provided the traveller with a leisurely, but scenic, journey punctuated by frequent stops at stylish stations serving bucolic villages. The example selected here is the East Grinstead–Lewes line, before it made any claim to fame as a pioneer site for rail

line preservation. Its counterparts were the appropriately named 'Cuckoo Line' linking Eridge and Polegate, the Eridge–Lewes via Uckfield section which survived partial truncation to assume a new commuter function, and the Christs Hospital–Shoreham-by-Sea link, which never attained its theoretical role as a diversionary route for the Brighton main line. Perhaps of lesser significance was the branch line which diverged from the electrified mid-Sussex route at Pulborough and headed in a westerly direction, carefully avoiding most population centres en route, until it joined the Portsmouth direct line at Petersfield in Hampshire. Lastly we visit one of the most obscure backwaters, the Chichester–Midhurst line, which clung to life for many years after the loss of its passenger service and, even in its final years, refused to go quietly.

In order to establish a firmer context for the photographic content, a table and map are offered to provide further guidance.

Sussex Railways 1950–2008, An Overview

	1950	2008	Change
Total Route Mileage	340.00	211.50	-128.50
Total Electrified Mileage	158.25	184.75	+ 26.50
Total Non Electrified Mileage	181.75	26.75	-153.00

During the period extending from 1950 to 2008, 131.75 route miles were closed, including four branches featured herein. As a partial offset, the development of the railway preservation movement concurrently resulted in the resurrection, for seasonal operation, of 16.25 miles of line which had been subject to earlier abandonment.

A Mecca for Maunsell Enthusiasts

The Hastings line was an early attempt by the South Eastern Railway (SER) to gain access to a rapidly developing section of the south coast bounded by Hastings, St Leonards and Bexhill. In strategic terms it was a successful attempt to contain further eastern expansion by the London, Brighton and South Coast Railway (LB&SCR) as it spread tentacles across Sussex. Southwards from Tunbridge Wells, in 1851 the new main line was completed within two years and the distinctive architectural style of William Tress, as embodied in the stations at Frant, Wadhurst, Witherenden (subsequently renamed Ticehurst Road and later Stonegate), Etchingham, Robertsbridge, and Battle enriched the rural landscape.

Wealden topography presented significant barriers for railway construction with the result that four necessary tunnels – Wadhurst (1,205 yards), Gore Hill (287 yards), Strawberry Hill (286 yards) and Mountfield (5,266 yards) inflated construction costs which totalled £725,000. In addition, ill advised efforts to minimise tunneling costs required rebuilding and the imposition of tight loading gauge restrictions that were to impede operations as far as locomotives and rolling stock were concerned, until electrification on 27 April 1986. At the coastal end of the line, SER trains shared the Bopeep (1,318 yards) and Hastings (788 yards) tunnels with those of the LB&SCR, which exercised running powers over that section. Curvature and variable gradient profiles further contributed to operating difficulties in the steam era. The solution chosen by the Southern Railway was to deploy the powerful three cylinder Schools class 4-4-0's, introduced by Maunsell between 1930 and 1935, on the Hastings line. The photographs will give some idea of the number of these superb locomotives that were in daily service during the fifties.

White elephant or Lost Opportunity?

After fifty years of service to Hastings and St Leonards, the SER was prompted to grasp the business challenge presented by rapid residential growth at Bexhill. The reaction of the company was initially spectacular, with the opening of a spacious new junction station at Crowhurst, between Battle and West St Leonards. From there a branch line diverged in a southwesterly direction over the massive seventeen-arch Crowhurst or Coombe Haven viaduct which consumed nine million bricks, attained a height of 67 feet and took twenty months to complete. This enormous investment ensured access to a terminus at Bexhill West where two island platforms with a length of 700 feet, together with extensive platform canopies and quite grandiose station buildings, were prepared to receive the anticipated multitude of travellers. The problem was that this boom in business never really materialised and, after its opening in 1902, through services to London lasted for only ten years. It is interesting to note that the fastest running time of Bexhill West to London Cannon Street through services were then about the same as those that prevail today between St Leonards Warrior Square and Cannon Street with electric traction. Thereafter, the Bexhill West branch settled down to a more humdrum existence with infrastructure far in excess of the traffic requirements. Two-coach push-pull trains and a daily goods working became the norm. In retrospect it is perhaps surprising that branch passenger services continued until 15 June 1964, since regular freight services ceased on 9 September 1963. At least it can be said that the branch went out with a bang as, following the lifting of track in July 1965, the viaduct was demolished by explosives in May 1969 and the station at Crowhurst was reduced thereafter to a more humble status.

In more recent times the Hastings line witnessed the introduction in 1958 of specially designed diesel-electric multiple units, known for their reliability and power, if not for their comfort and aesthetic design. Electrification followed in 1986, and loading gauge limitation in the tunnels was mitigated by the singling of track within. Today the line, with its steadily increasing number of commuters, is well served by a steady stream of Class 375 Electrostars. Unfortunately lineside vegetation control economies by Network Rail make the enjoyment of the beautiful Wealden countryside increasingly difficult.

The Bluebell is a Resilient Flower

The story of the resurrection of a part of the former East Grinstead to Lewes line as the Bluebell Railway has been an ongoing saga since 1959 that will deservedly retain a time honoured place in the annals of the heritage rail movement in Britain. What is now more easily overlooked is its earlier history as a Wealden railway backwater which, after a relatively uneventful existence, did not calmly fade away in response to the dictates of the rationalizers on the British Railways Board. Opened in 1882, it was always notable for the bucolic scenery with which it blended so well and the splendour of its intermediate stations, which were extraordinarily generous in scale given their distance from population centres.

For much of its life, the line typified other LB&SCR backwaters in Sussex pursuing a low profile role, connecting the countryside to the commercial centres at each end with a relatively infrequent and leisurely passenger service which sufficed until the bus and then the car transformed rural travel patterns, and a modest freight role which addressed the needs of the rural economy. The quite extensive junction at Horsted Keynes was the terminus for one of the oddest electric services operated by the Southern, a relic of unfulfilled expansion plans interrupted by World War II, and the author has fond memories of journeying in an empty 2NOL unit from there to Seaford via Ardingly, Haywards Heath and Lewes.

This was the ambience that the writer encountered and relished on his early visits in the fifties. It all seemed too good to last and it nearly didn't. Services from East Grinstead to Lewes were initially withdrawn on 28 May 1955, but this was by no means the final chapter. Enter Margery Bessemer, a resident of Chailey, whose researches revealed clauses in the original act that required that the line could be closed only by Act of Parliament and not at the will of the railway. Furthermore, that the stations of West Hoathly, Newick and Chailey and Sheffield Park were similarly protected. The subsequent litigation upheld these legal requirements, with the result that a limited statutory service of four trains each way, usually consisting of one coach, was reinstated to the stations specified as well as Horsted Keynes. Through ticketing arrangements beyond the line were also cancelled in order to further discourage patronage. This strictly constructionist approach heralded what was known locally as the 'sulky service' which was widely viewed as a begrudging response by a government under pressure. It was not surprising that this respite lasted only from 7 August 1956 until Parliament extinguished the rights, effective 17 March 1958. By this time the case had become something of a cause célèbre and the writer was part of the throng aboard the last journey from Lewes to East Grinstead. Perhaps it would be appropriate one day for the Bluebell Railway to consider commemorating the effort of Margery Bessemer by conferring her name upon a locomotive!

The photographs deliberately omit most of the more familiar locations on the Bluebell Railway, which because of their use by so many film and TV production companies and continuing attention in the railway press, will be familiar to readers. Instead the focus is mainly on locations that have now disappeared and are permanently beyond the reach of the preservationists. Today the station at Barcombe survives as a residence while housing development now covers the site of Newick & Chailey station and the station buildings at West Hoathly have been demolished.

Off the Beaten Track to Midhurst

It is a curious fact that the beginnings of this east–west aligned cross country byway originated as an extension of a line from Horsham to the general vicinity of the town of Petworth in 1859. It soon became the poor relation of a reorientated main line to Arundel and the coast. Its westward expansion was limited by an agreement between the LB&SCR and L&SWR

which set the small town of Midhurst as the demarcation line between the spheres of interest of the two companies. For the first seven years of its existence a station named Petworth, but actually located at Coultershaw Bridge one and half miles south of the town, was the terminus. In October 1866 the train service was extended via Selham and a 276 yard tunnel to Midhurst which, with a population of less than two thousand, offered meagre traffic generation prospects. In the same year the L&SWR arrived with a line from Petersfield and established a separate station, goods facilities and loco shed at Midhurst.

Until the 1923 grouping and the creation of the Southern Railway, Midhurst continued to enjoy, or perhaps endure, this duplication of facilities which was probably a doubtful blessing as far as the travelling public and goods shippers were concerned. Stations on the Pulborough to Midhurst section were modest by LB&SCR standards, with timber being the preferred building material, although a somewhat larger wooden structure replaced the original station at Petworth in 1892 probably in deference to it being the railhead for Petworth Park, the seat of Lord Leconfield. The opening of the line from Chichester to Midhurst in 1881 saw the adoption of a form of 'stockbroker Tudor' architectural style at Midhurst and south to the cathedral city. Generally, the line from Petersfield was conceived as a feeder to the Portsmouth direct line and its stations were relatively unpretentious, whereas the LB&SCR briefly entertained thoughts of transforming the Pulborough–Midhurst–Chichester connection into a main line to Portsmouth.

In the fifties most trains ran through from Pulborough to Petersfield and the Drummond M7s from Guildford shed were not unduly challenged by the one- or two-coach push-pull trains which sufficed for the few travellers who presented themselves at the inconveniently located stations. Passenger services ceased on 5 February 1955 when the Midhurst–Petersfield section was closed to all traffic. The remainder of the line continued to wither on the vine for several more years, with freight services being withdrawn from Fittleworth and Selham in May 1963, Midhurst in October 1964 and finally from Petworth in

May 1966, ending 107 years of freight service at the original terminus. Enjoying the undoubted charm of this branch line was all too often a solitary pleasure and the longevity of its passenger service was quite an enigma – perhaps it was an out-of-sight out-of-mind situation, where the authorities were concerned!

The Forgotten Route to Goodwood

As sometimes occurs in railway history, the last route to reach Midhurst was destined to be the first to be abandoned, although the short southern section linking Chichester and Lavant outlived the other Midhurst lines. The line possessed some notable engineering work necessitated by a need to overcome the barrier presented by the South Downs. There were three tunnels – at West Dean (445 yards), Singleton (741 yards) and Cocking (738 yards). The three stations at Lavant, Singleton and Cocking were all impressive 'stockbroker Tudor' style structures. Singleton was exceptional in that it possessed two island platforms, a refreshment room and VIP facilities for the royal train, a yard capable of accommodating up to fourteen special trains, two signal boxes and water columns, a water tower and goods shed. The quite lavish provision of passenger facilities was designed to meet the occasional surge in traffic generated by race meetings at nearby Goodwood.

Apart from the race traffic, local demand for passenger services was very limited and they ceased in 1935. The line continued to handle a significant, but declining, volume of freight traffic and during World War II its tunnels provided an occasional refuge from aerial attack for ammunition trains destined for Portsmouth naval dockyard. In November 1951 the collapse of a culvert between Cocking and Midhurst resulted in a fiery derailment of the daily freight train from Chichester. In August 1953 the line was cut back to Lavant and goods services were withdrawn from Singleton and Cocking. The writer was privileged to walk the entire length of the line in 1954 and to ride the freight train from Chichester to Lavant in 1958. There was an undoubted fascination and some surprises in exploring the abandoned section. The condition of the tunnels was not too reassuring given the occasional bricks that had fallen from the tunnel linings and reliance on a torch, plus a degree of caution, was necessary. Singleton presented an extraordinary scene with station platforms retaining buildings and canopies, albeit in a very dilapidated condition. The real surprise was the discovery of a LB&SCR wheelbarrow, resplendent in Stroudley's 'improved engine green' livery and bearing the additional title 'Petworth Loco Department'. This raised questions in the author's mind that have not been satisfactorily resolved during the succeeding fifty years. Did the wheelbarrow date from the 1859–66 period, when locomotives were presumably serviced at the Petworth terminus? Was there a loco shed at Petworth at that time? If so, no record of its existence has been discovered. Lastly there is the ongoing question as to the fate of this notable relic. Does it still exist and if so where? Perhaps readers can throw some light upon this mystery.

My later visit to Lavant was another extraordinary experience. Arriving at Chichester with a brake van pass, I was directed to the yard where I was assured the train waited. However it transpired that, since no traffic was on offer, it was not planned to run to Lavant that day. My unexpected appearance changed all that and the train crew agreed that my properly authorized presence was enough to justify a special journey with provision for photo stops on request en route. This was the only occasion that I enjoyed the privilege of a private train in Britain. Lavant functioned until 1970 as a regional centre for the loading of sugar beet but its last task was handling an intensive shuttle movement of locally extracted gravel from a loading hopper situated to the south of Lavant station to a plant east of Chichester for washing and screening. Finally closure took place in 1991 and the Lavant section is now followed by a trail known as the Centurions Way. Lavant station was subsequently converted to flats while the station houses at Singleton and Cocking have been adapted for commercial and residential uses. The mouldering remains on the platforms at Singleton are now but a distant memory. It is doubtful whether many of the crowds who flock to 'glorious Goodwood' are aware that their predecessors, once upon a time, arrived in style by train.

With a population of approximately 4,900 in 2001, Midhurst, in spite of its history as a focal point of three rail routes, was clearly a small community to achieve the significance it attained on the railway map. All traces of the former LB&SCR station there have vanished under a housing development.

Acknowledgements

Once again the author wishes to express his gratitude for the photographic contributions of Gerald Siviour and the technical assistance of Michael Bowie of Lux Photographic Services, Carleton Place, Ontario.

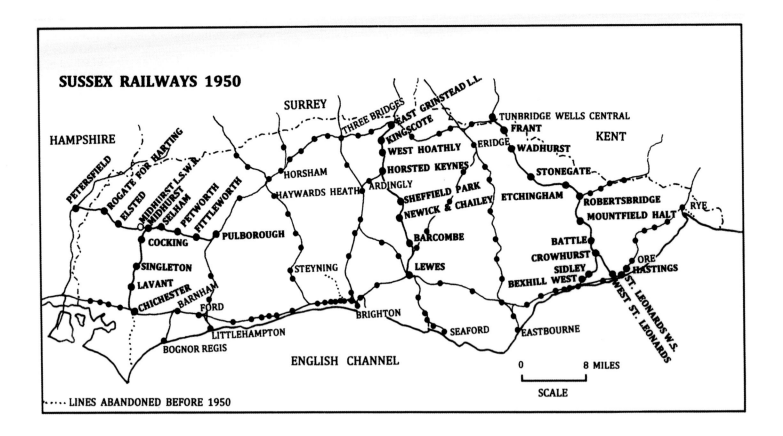

Tunbridge Wells Central–Hastings Main Line

Schools class No 30917 *Ardingly* pauses at the staggered platforms at Frant on 16 April 1957 with a Hastings–Tonbridge local train. Frant was one of the original stations designed by SER architect William Tress for the opening of the line in 1851. Its attractive gothic ragstone building, like its larger counterpart at Battle, was awarded a Grade II listed designation in 1982. The growth in commuter traffic in the decades following the fifties saved this delightful station from closure.

Wadhurst, seen here on 9 April 1956, is a classic William Tress country station in which brick replaced stone as building material. Note the absence of protection from the elements on the down side, whilst typical SER wooden buildings and canopy shelter London commuters on the up platform. Further inspiration for the modeller is provided by an ensemble consisting of a typical footbridge, goods shed and sidings.

GR Siviour

Schools class 4-4-0 No 30902 *Wellington* leaves Wadhurst on 9 April 1956 with a three coach birdcage set of appropriate SER ancestry forming an all stations up service. Most trains on the Hastings line ran on fairly leisurely schedules during the fifties which afforded the traveller an opportunity to enjoy the distinctive three cylinder music of a Schools in action.

GR Siviour

On home territory, an elderly L class 4-4-0 calls at Etchingham with a Tunbridge Wells Central–Hastings stopping train on 6 August 1956.

Bullied's unlovely, but reliable, utility class Q1s put in occasional appearances on the Hastings line. Here No 33035 passes Etchingham at speed on 6 August 1956 with a Charing Cross–Hastings service.

Right: The more adventurous traveller who ventured off the main line at Robertsbridge onto the Kent & East Sussex line would soon encounter the oddly named halt known as 'Junction Road for Hawkhurst', photographed on 2 January 1954. Serving hopfields rather than habitation, it would be interesting to speculate if any geographically challenged travellers destined for Hawkhurst were ever tempted to alight there for a wearisome six mile trudge to the town. The choice of 'Junction Road' suggested a slightly desperate grasping for relevant toponomy in the best light railway tradition.

Left: Mountfield Halt, seen here on 6 August 1956, was the last station to be opened on the Hastings line and the first to be closed. Its sleeper built platforms lit by paraffin lamps survived for forty-six years until passenger service was withdrawn on 6 October 1969. Three quarters of mile north of Mountfield is the junction of the branch serving a gypsum mine which ceased operations in 1990. However the plasterboard plant at the mine site survived and then used gypsum derived until recently by conveyor from a mine at nearby Brightling and by train from northern power stations such as Drax, where it was a product of the desulphurization process. Currently imported French gypsum is conveyed on a daily basis by GB Railfreight from Southampton. The halt was located immediately south of a level crossing replete with an SER crossing keepers house. The only reminder of the halt that remains today is a nameboard which adorns a garden furniture shop housed in a nearby former Methodist chapel.

Notwithstanding its lowly status as the least used and most unpretentious station on the Hastings line, Mountfield Halt was linked to London by Pullman service. Here, on 6 August 1956, Schools class No 30928 *Stowe* adds dignity and grace to the rural setting as it pauses at the empty platform with a down train. This locomotive, which put in thirty eight years of service accumulating more than one million miles, is now the property of the Maunsell Locomotive Society and is based at Sheffield Park on the Bluebell Railway where it is on static display pending restoration to running order.

Schools No 30906 *Sherbourne* speeds past Mountfield Halt with an up train on 6 August 1956. The inclusion of non corridor stock on some Hastings line services continued until the replacement of steam by diesel-electric multiple units in 1958.

Battle station represented the finest expression of the gothic style favoured by Tress on the Hastings line. Here Schools No 30939 *Leatherhead* approaches the staggered platforms with a Hastings to Charing Cross train on a hot summers day, 6 August 1956.

Schools No 30924 *Haileybury*, with a Hastings train, passes beneath the lofty road bridge midway between Battle and Crowhurst on 6 August 1956.

Right: Crowhurst formerly boasted fine station buildings that reflected its importance as a main line junction when it was opened in 1902. Today only the small brick lamp room on the left survives as a peak hour ticket office while passengers are offered the limited protection of bus shelters.

To complete this scene of retrenchment, the layout has been reduced to two tracks and the signal box has been removed.

Left: By contrast, Crowhurst presented a vastly different scene in the fifties when both of its Bexhill West branch bay platforms were occupied by H class 0-4-4Ts operating push-pull services, as on 6 August 1956.

As seen from the footbridge, the view south towards the junction of the Bexhill West branch, and the main line south to West St Leonards, was an impressive reminder of the confident aspirations of the SER in the days before road competition.

L class 4-4-0 No 31771, built in 1914 by Beyer Peacock, stops at Crowhurst, on 6 August 1956, with a down train while passengers change for the Bexhill West branch. This locomotive was destined to survive for a further five years before it was withdrawn for scrapping.

The wooden weatherboard buildings of West St Leonards station reverberate to the mellifluous sounds of coupling rods as a Schools class 4-4-0 rounds the sharp curve from Bopeep Junction on a Hastings–Charing Cross train on 6 August 1956.

Standard class 4 2-6-0 No 76060 prepares to make an unheralded departure from Hastings with the last regularly scheduled steam service for Charing Cross, on 8 June 1958.

On 8 June 1958 a Schools class 4-4-0 waits at Hastings with rolling stock that is definitely not 'Restriction O' and obviously did not arrive from the Tunbridge Wells line. Note the narrower Hastings stock and Pullmans berthed in the yard beyond. All has now changed at Hastings. This scene was transformed by the erection of new station buildings on the site in 2004.

Standard class 2MT 2-6-2T No 84028 and an unidentified Schools class double head an Ashford train entering Ore on 8 June 1958. At the time, all electric services terminated at Ore, the adjacent electric car sheds were busy and the station buildings were extant. Decay is pervasive there today.

Crowhurst–Bexhill West Branch

On 8 June 1958 a Crowhurst push-pull train stops at the intermediate branch station of Sidley where the platform shelters had a marked resemblance to sports pavilions.

On the same date, an H class 0-4-4T propels a Crowhurst–Bexhill West train away from Sidley towards the quite extensive goods yard for the last half mile to the terminus.

Left: The original station building at Sidley had been converted to a BP service station before the fifties. It is seen here on 8 June 1958. Strangely enough this structure was subsequently replaced by a more modern facility at the same site.

Below: On 10 August 1953, an immaculate Wainwright H class 0-4-4T No 31295 leaves Bexhill West with a Crowhurst train.

One of the rapidly vanishing Billinton D3 class 0-4-4Ts, No 32384, is about to leave the commodious terminus at Bexhill West with a return branch working to Crowhurst on 10 August 1953. The locomotive was withdrawn shortly after this photograph was taken.

Built to handle anticipated crowds of holidaymakers that never materialized, the station at Bexhill West was usually a destination for two-coach push-pull services in its later years, although Maunsell stock was frequently stabled there due to the inadequate siding accommodation at Hastings. This view shows it on 10 August 1953.

Left: Bexhill West on 8 June 1958. In its final years, it was obviously far too large for the traffic on offer and the grass that was encroaching upon the platforms added to the melancholy atmosphere. The platforms have now been demolished and the former goods yard is an industrial estate.

Right: From the forecourt on the same date, the station buildings at Bexhill West echoed the determination of the SER to assert a strong presence in the heart of LB&SCR territory. After closure the station survived, with some modifications, as an auction hall. A portion, which began life in the SER era as a restaurant operated by Spiers & Ponds Ltd, continues to provide sustenance under the somewhat ironic title 'Doctor Beechings'.

East Grinstead–Lewes

The last surviving D3 class 0-4-4T No 32390 at East Grinstead Low Level station, on 10 October 1953, with an RCTS special that started from Three Bridges and followed a route which is now mostly lost via East Grinstead High Level, Eridge, Polegate, Lewes, East Grinstead Low Level before terminating at Three Bridges. The Station at East Grinstead is now much changed with the fine LB&SCR station buildings replaced by an ugly brutalist style concrete structure and the high level platforms, visible in the background have been demolished.

On 16 March 1958 Standard class 4MT 2-6-4T No 80154 leaves East Grinstead Low Level with the crowded last train for Lewes. Note the symbolism of the wilted bluebell that adorns the locomotive. Current indications suggest that it will be a little more than fifty years following this closure date, before the first restored Bluebell Railway passenger service passes this way.

Also on the last day of services, No 80011, with a greatly augmented train, passes the silent and ignored station of Kingscote with an Lewes to East Grinstead service.

The station at West Hoathly did not survive the closure and subsequent reincarnation of the line as the Bluebell Railway. Whereas other stations between Sheffield Park and Kingscote were gradually reopened, the demolition of the buildings in 1967 at West Hoathly prevented a resumption of service there. Sharpthorne tunnel is visible to the south of the station in this view on 9 April 1955.

On 9 April 1955 Ivatt class 2MT 2-6-2T No 41259 pauses beneath the weather beaten glazed footbridge at West Hoathly with a Brighton train.

On 16 March 1958 Standard class 4MT 2-6-4T No 80011, one of a batch of ten built at Doncaster between 1951 and 1956, leaves West Hoathly with a Lewes train on the last day of operations.

An extensive panorama of West Hoathly station and the line extending north towards Kingscote from above the north portal of Sharpthorne tunnel, on the same date.

With the recent focus upon the activities of the Bluebell Railway at Horsted Keynes, it is often forgotten that this generously proportioned country junction was also once an outpost of the Southern electric network. Here, on 9 April 1955, an elderly NOL unit, No 1826, is inspected as the tail lamp is removed. The NOL units were converted from LSWR steam stock between 1934 and 1936. Headcode 37 denoted an all stations service to Seaford via Ardingly, Haywards Heath and Lewes. The advent of World War II prevented the extension of electrification north of Horsted Keynes and the link to Haywards Heath was closed to all traffic between Horsted Keynes and Ardingly on 28 October 1963. It was odd that the only electrified platform at Horsted Keynes in the 1950's was bereft of any protection from the elements.

Long term plans for restoration of the route to Ardingly have been discussed by the Bluebell Railway, although this will not include reinstallation of an energised conductor rail.

South of Sheffield Park the wooded Wealden countryside has not been disturbed by the passage of trains for the last fifty years. On the final day, 16 March 1958, No 80111 approaches Newick and Chailey with an East Grinstead–Lewes service.

On 9 April 1955 Class 4MT 2-6-4T No 80019 leaves Newick and Chailey with a Brighton–Victoria train composed of vintage rolling stock.

The massive tile hung station building at Newick and Chailey was connected to the platform by a covered stairway. A funereal atmosphere prevailed on the last day in this view south towards Barcombe. The scene is now covered by a housing development.

Left: The yard at Newick and Chailey had been cleared of wagons in readiness for closure, as No 80011 makes a vigorous start en route to Lewes with a train from East Grinstead on the last day of operation on the 'Bluebell' line, 16 March 1958.

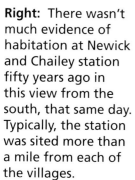

Right: There wasn't much evidence of habitation at Newick and Chailey station fifty years ago in this view from the south, that same day. Typically, the station was sited more than a mile from each of the villages.

Historically there must have been an obstreperous landowner who insisted on construction of the short tunnel at Cinder Hill, between Newick and Chailey and Barcombe, seen here on the last operating day. The tunnel provided a refuge from air attack on one occasion during World War II.

At the southern, and now dismantled, extremity of the Bluebell line ex-LB&SCR C2X class 0-6-0 No 32440 (a 1911 rebuild by Marsh of a Billinton C2 built by Vulcan Foundry in 1893) stops at Barcombe with a three coach birdcage set forming an East Grinstead–Lewes football supporters train on 9 April 1955. This locomotive was withdrawn in 1958.

Left: Barcombe station was unusual in having only one platform. The village was about one mile distant, and at the time, had the distinction of being served by two stations. The other, Barcombe Mills, subsequently lost its train service when the line from Lewes to Uckfield was closed on 4 May 1969. Here Ivatt class 2MT 2-6-2T No 41259 is approaching with a Brighton–Oxted train on 9 April 1955.

Right: U1 class 3 cylinder 2-6-0 No 31902, rebuilt at Eastleigh in 1931 from a River class 2-6-4T, is approaching Culver Junction with a Victoria–Brighton, via Sheffield Park, train on the same day. To the right can be seen the line to Uckfield and Eridge. Little remains of the railways at the site of Culver Junction today.

Pulborough–Midhurst–Petersfield

M7 0-4-4T No 30049 and its solitary push-pull coach provides a connection with the electric services at Pulborough on 4 December 1954.

M7 0-4-4T No 30051 pauses at Fittleworth with a Pulborough–Midhurst push-pull train on 19 April 1954. The absence of passengers allowed an exchange of pleasantries between the porter and the guard.

Left: Fittleworth station on 4 December 1954, looking east towards Hardham Junction and Pulborough. Fittleworth was opened on 2 September 1889, thirty years after the line first saw trains. Its signal box survived until 1931. Closure to passengers took place on 7 February 1955 but freight traffic was handled until 6 May 1963, although goods trains continued to pass by en route from Pulborough to Petworth until 1966.

Right: The wooden SER style station at Fittleworth, seen here from the forecourt on the same day, overlooked the water meadows of the River Rother almost one mile south of the village. The goods yard was quite a hive of activity on this occasion with a farmer loading outgoing sugar beets and the coal merchant unloading and bagging incoming coal. Closure at Fittleworth was followed by a period of decay during which part of the platform was demolished before the station building was restored as a residence which still exists.

Left: M7 0-4-4T No 30051 trundles a Midhurst–Pulborough train across the fields near Shopham Bridge between Petworth and Fittleworth on 19 April 1954.

Below: On the same date, M7 No 30047 leaves Petworth on a Pulborough train as the signalman returns to the signal box with the tablet for the Midhurst–Petworth section.

Top: Petworth was the first railhead for the Midhurst area, with services from Horsham commencing on 10 October 1859. It ceased to be a terminus in October 1866 when the line was extended to Midhurst. The small town of Petworth was almost two miles distant to the north, as was the seat of Lord Leconfield at Petworth Park, to whom the LB&SCR accorded due recognition by replacing the original station with a slightly more impressive, albeit wooden, structure in 1892. Sixty two years later, on 4 December 1954, this second station at Petworth had a forlorn appearance and was sadly in need of a repaint. Surprisingly, after closure the ongoing rot was eventually reversed and the modest residence it had become was transformed into The Old Railway Station Guest House where four retired Pullman cars previously at Marazion stand on the former trackbed.

Bottom: On the same day, time was running out for the passenger service as M7 0-4-4T No 30049 paused at the neglected station at Petworth with a Pulborough train. The platform canopy was shortened in 1932 after a clearance of nesting bees which had made life difficult for passengers.

On 4 December 1954, M7 0-4-4T No 30028 propels a Pulborough to Midhurst push-pull train into the deserted and isolated station at Selham. Note the separate road access to the cattle dock. The nearby hamlet and pub were doubtless meagre sources of business although some residual coal traffic survived until May 1963.

M7 No 30047 waits for the photographer at Selham, en route from Pulborough with a push-pull working for Midhurst on 19 April 1954. The wooden station building dated from 1872 and after closure became a residence. The signal box here was abolished in 1933. Note the cattle dock which is just visible to the left of the locomotive.

Left: The wooden station buildings at Selham, Petworth and Fittleworth were quite unusual for the LB&SCR and would have looked more at home on the SER in Kent. It would appear that a shipment of bricks has recently arrived by rail at Selham in this eastward view towards Petworth on 4 December 1954.

Right: Making a steamy exit from Midhurst on a windy day, M7 tank No 30028 heads towards the tunnel with a Pulborough train, also on 4 December 1954. Traces of the former quarry sidings are visible in the foreground.

The attractive tile hung station at Midhurst is graced by M7 No 30028 awaiting departure with a Pulborough train on the same date. The only vital ingredients that are missing from this time honoured scene are the throngs of passengers who long since had transferred their allegiance to the hourly bus service to Haslemere station and the Southdown direct coach service to London.

Midhurst on 4 December 1954. The LB&SCR station here provided generous accommodation for the modest one- or two-coach push-pull sets that were more the than adequate for passenger requirements during the line's final decades of existence. The bay platform on the left was the domain of some Petersfield services. Now the station site has been obliterated by housing development and trains are but a fading memory for some of the towns older inhabitants.

On the same date, M7 0-4-4T No 30028 is approaching Midhurst with a Petersfield–Pulborough train. In the foreground is the line to Chichester on which the remaining freight service between Midhurst and Cocking had been withdrawn following a culvert collapse and subsequent train wreck on 19 November 1951. To the right of the locomotive is the site of the second LB&SCR loco shed built in 1907. Beyond, some of the Midhurst goods facilities are just discernible.

The LSWR was first on the scene at Midhurst, with its line from Petersfield opening two years ahead of the LB&SCR on 1 September 1864. A freight connection between the two stations was established on 17 December 1866, but passenger services did not link the two lines until a weak bridge at Bepton Road was replaced on 12 July 1925, by the Southern Railway. This permitted the closure of the LSWR station, which nonetheless continued to survive in commercial use and remains to this day. On 4 December 1954 it was in remarkably good condition although its platform canopy had been cut back.

Two views of Elsted station on 4 December 1954:

Left: Elsted station was situated one and a half miles northwest of the village it was intended to serve. The sober brick building with rendering was supplemented by a corrugated iron goods shed and lamp room and was very similar in design to the LSWR stations at Rogate and Midhurst. The dimensions of the road bridge to the west of the station suggest the former existence of a passing loop that was probably removed at an early date.

Right: Elsted station from the forecourt. The station building was demolished after closure and the site has now been redeveloped for industrial purposes.

A Midhurst–Petersfield push-pull service powered by one of the regular M7's, No 30028, drifts slowly into the deserted platform at Elsted on 4 December 1954. The sombre weather conditions seem strangely appropriate as only two months remained before the Midhurst–Petersfield section was to be closed to all traffic. Note the generous provision of fire buckets, the water tank on the roof of the gents and the paucity of platform lighting.

Rogate for Harting station was inconveniently situated between the villages for which it was named and, during its later years, should more appropriately have been rechristened Nyewood for the community that sprung up around it. It retained the only signal box, housing a ground frame, and possessed the only passing loop on the Midhurst–Petersfield section, although only one platform was in regular use at the end. As is evident on 4 December 1954, the line struck out boldly from here across thinly populated country to the east in the direction of Elsted. The chimney of a small sawmill is visible on the left.

On 4 December 1954 M7 No 30028 calls at Rogate for Harting with a Petersfield–Midhurst train to pick up three passengers. Note the somewhat woebegone condition of the signal box. Beyond the bridge was a siding serving the Nyewood brickworks.

Chichester–Midhurst

The disused station at Cocking is seen on 19 April 1954. Cocking was officially closed to goods traffic on 28 August 1953, after serving as the northern terminus of the line from Chichester since 19 November 1951, when a culvert south of Midhurst was washed out, causing an embankment to collapse with serious and fiery consequences for C2X class 0-6-0 No 32522, working the 09.30 goods from Chichester. A sleeper marking the temporary limit of train working is visible at the north end of the platform. At one time there was a signal box at the southern end of the platform. This, the least used station on the line, has been modified as a residence.

Singleton on 19 April 1954. In the days of passenger traffic the two island platforms at Singleton witnessed moments of glory as crowds of race goers, destined for Goodwood, descended on it in special trains. Its peaceful setting amidst the folds of the South Downs was for most of the year unsullied by such intrusions. During the final eighteen years after the loss of passenger services in 1935, with the exception of a period during the second world war when the nearby tunnels provided an occasional refuge for ammunition trains destined for the Royal Navy base at Portsmouth, the tranquillity of Singleton was disturbed by nothing more than a daily goods train. The station house is visible at a lower level in the right background, while in the foreground is a hint of the water tower and a glimpse of the mysterious wheelbarrow referred to in the text. After closure the yard was used by a scrap merchant, while the station house became a reception centre for the Chilsdown winery.

Lavant on 27 May 1959. E4 0-6-2T No 32509 has just run around its train, which on this occasion was run solely for the benefit of the writer, before returning to Chichester. The limit of train operations at Lavant can be seen beyond the loop together with the extensive concrete platform for sugar beet loading situated north of the imposing station building, which was subsequently divided into multiple dwelling units.

An advantage of having a 'private' train was that the friendly crew made photo stops as required. Here, E4 No 32509 makes a photo stop north of Chichester on the Lavant branch. The contemporary scene is much changed with the northerly expansion of the city and the conversion of the rail right-of-way to a hiking trail known as the 'Centurians Way'.